Footsteps in the Dust

Advent Poems and Prayers

Thom M. Shuman

Footsteps in the Dust

Copyright © 2015 Thom M. Shuman

All rights reserved.

ISBN: 1517326060
ISBN-13: 978-1517326067

DEDICATION

We have never met this side of life,
but her example of faithful service,
of caring for all of God's creatures,
of seeing the good in every person
and seeing in every person the image of God,
has impacted my life and ministry.

As we await the promised advent
which will gather together
all of God's beloved
who have followed Jesus'
footsteps in the dust,

this book is for my colleague in ministry,

Paula Morse.

Throughout the centuries, artists have shared their visions of what that journey to Bethlehem must have been like. Stargazers have wondered what the heavens may have held to signal such a momentous birth. Families use advent calendars to tell the story as the season unfolds, or populate manger sets with the familiar shepherds, kings, angels, sheep, and family (as well as dogs, cats, dinosaurs, and occasionally action figures beloved by children).

These poems and prayers are my thoughts about this holy season. My hope is that you might find them to faithful companions on your journey.

Table of Contents

First Sunday of Advent	*all i want for Christmas*	2
First Monday of Advent	*bethphage*	3
First Tuesday of Advent	*here, there, everywhere*	4
First Wednesday of Advent	*footsteps in the dust*	5
First Thursday of Advent	*you could*	6
First Friday of Advent	*the end*	8
First Saturday of Advent	*heads or tails*	9
Second Sunday of Advent	*teacher*	10
Second Monday of Advent	*splendiferous*	11
Second Tuesday of Advent	*which?*	12
Second Wednesday of Advent	*the oath*	14
Second Thursday of Advent	*neglect*	16
Second Friday of Advent	*praise!*	17
Second Saturday of Advent	*now*	18
Third Sunday of Advent	*students*	19
Third Monday of Advent	*tetchy*	20
Third Tuesday of Advent	*searching*	21
Third Wednesday of Advent	*blankly*	22
Third Thursday of Advent	*the elect*	23
Third Friday of Advent	*inheritance*	24
Third Saturday of Advent	*in every season*	26
Fourth Sunday of Advent	*i'm dreaming of*	27
Fourth Monday of Advent	*impatiently*	28
Fourth Tuesday of Advent	*freedom*	30
Fourth Wednesday of Advent	*advent eyes*	32
Fourth Thursday of Advent	*so many*	33
Fourth Friday of Advent	*but*	34
Christmas Eve	*night silence*	35
Christmas Day	*one*	36

all i want for Christmas

The word that Isaiah son of Amoz saw concerning Judah and Jerusalem.
In days to come the mountain of the LORD's house shall be established
   as the highest of the mountains,
and shall be raised above the hills;
   all the nations shall stream to it.
Many peoples shall come and say,
   "Come, let us go up to the mountain of the LORD,
   to the house of the God of Jacob;
that he may teach us his ways
   and that we may walk in his paths." (Isaiah 2:1-3)

communities which spend more to lift families out of poverty
   than they do on tax breaks for corporations;

politicians who give as much time to soup kitchens and shelters
   as they do to $1000-a-plate fundraisers;

stores which pay their salespeople a fairer wage,
   as they reduce the perks and bonuses of management;

neighbors who notice the old couple struggling
to walk their rescued dogs,
   and rush to take the leashes for them;

military forces which spend more time building bridges
   than blowing up infrastructures;

churches which care more for their communities
   than putting butts in the pews;

my ability to give away two (or more) items
to those in true need
   for every one I receive (and don't really need);

that's my Christmas list for this year.

First Sunday of Advent

bethphage

When they had come near Jerusalem and had reached Bethphage, at the Mount of Olives, Jesus sent two disciples, saying to them, "Go into the village ahead of you, and immediately you will find a donkey tied, and a colt with her; untie them and bring them to me. If anyone says anything to you, just say this, 'The Lord needs them.' And he will send them immediately." (Matthew 21:1-3)

    the poor would
      become philanthropists;

    little children
      would become our teachers;

    the voiceless
      would be the guest speakers;

    the broken
      would become healers of us all;

    hatred could
      not gain a foothold in our hearts;

    misery could
      not find a home anywhere;

    evil would
      become an extinct species;

    compassion would
      be second nature;

    love would
      be our constant companion

    if we would go and do as
        you

    direct us.

    First Monday of Advent

here, there, everywhere

Therefore I intend to keep on reminding you of these things, though you know them already and are established in the truth that has come to you.
(2 Peter 1:12)

there
  in the pint-sized girl who
    stands up to the
        playground bully,
     i recall
        that you always
        take the side
  of the most
    vulnerable;

here
  in the store as
    the woman ahead of me
    slowly counts her money
    to see if she can buy all she needs for her child,
    and the stranger
    just ahead of her hands the cashier
    a wad of bills whispering,
        'this should cover her bill,
        give her whatever is left,'
  i am given a cue
    as to how those who are blessed
    are called to live;

when the teenager
  gets up an hour early
    to shovel the snow-mantled sidewalks
  of his elderly neighbors
  before standing in morning's
        obscurity
    waiting for the school bus,
  memories of another
      Servant
    are stirred up.

here, there, everywhere, whenever,
keep on reminding me . . .

First Tuesday of Advent

footsteps in the dust

Thus says the LORD: As the shepherd rescues from the mouth of the lion two legs, or a piece of an ear, so shall the people of Israel who live in Samaria be rescued, with the corner of a couch and part of a bed. (Amos 3:12)

  when
      we have fallen into
    the pit, the walls
        as slick as glass
           and everyone
           walking by
           tosses platitudes
           down to us,
      you jump in
      and grab our hands,
  saying,
           'trust me,
        i know the way out;'

  when
      we are caught in
    sin's enticement, you
        firmly grasp its
           jaws,
      prying them apart
        until we can
        pull free;

  when
      we are waylaid
    by death, wrapped
  in its cold embrace,
        you shine a
           Light
      so we can see
      the footsteps
        in the dust
           which lead us
              to
  you.

First Wednesday of Advent

you could

In my distress I called upon the
    LORD;
  to my God I cried for help.
From his temple he heard my
    voice,
  and my cry to him reached his
    ears.

He brought me out into a broad
    place;
  he delivered me, because he
    delighted in me. (Psalm 18:6, 19)

you could level
    the mountains you shawled
        in snow
    to get our attention,

but you
  bend down to take
  sin's pebbles
    from our shoes;

you could send
    winter's wind,
      to rattle our
     windows
    to get our attention,

but you
  caress us with
  a cool breeze on
    the hottest of days;

you could push a
    wave to knock us off
        our pious pedestals,

but you
  hold a cup of water
    to our parched
     lips;

you could do anything,
              and everything,
  to deliver us,

but instead,

      you became

    us.

First Thursday of Advent

the end

*I keep the LORD always
 before me;
because he is at my
 right hand, I shall not be
 moved.* (Psalm 16:8)

if you walked
  in my
shadow,
    you might
    not be able
      to see
    what i am doing;

if you stayed
  (a very respectful)
    3 paces behind   me,
  then i would know
      who is who
      in this
    relationship;

if you came
    trailing after
        me,
  you could pick up the
      hurtful words,
      broken promises,
      missed opportunities
        i litter on my
          journey;

      but
if i let
      you
    lead,
  i know
  i will find
      my way
    to the
        end.

First Friday of Advent

heads or tails

Then he said to them, "Whose head is this, and whose title?" They answered, "The emperor's." Then he said to them, "Give therefore to the emperor the things that are the emperor's, and to God the things that are God's." (Matthew 22:20-21)

as the haves
    get haveier
  and the nots
    get notier,
i read of your
  heart breaking
      for the poor;

as the powerful
   stockpile more and more,
  and the vulnerable
    grow weaker and weaker,
   you speak of me giving away
     everything i have;

as the spin doctors
   talk louder and faster,
  and the voiceless
    can find no advocates,
   i hear your words
   of the last becoming
       first.

when i look at you,
wondering
    which side to take,
    which way to go,
  you take a coin
  out of your
      pocket
   and flipping it
   into the air, whisper,

'you call it'

First Saturday of Advent

teacher

Make me to know your
    ways, O LORD;
  teach me your paths.
Lead me in your truth, and
    teach me,
  for you are the God of my
    salvation;
  for you I wait all day long.   (Psalm 25:4-5)

taking the figures
    and moving them
        around
  on the flannel board
    you show us
    how the kingdom
  is to look;

stepping to the blackboard,
    you take the chalk
    from the student
trying to solve the equation
$(7 \times 7) - 3 \times 49 \div 5 \times 7 \times 7 \times 7 =$
  you write in ∞
    whispering, 'that's
    how many times you are
  to
    forgive.'

sitting us down
   in a semi-circle
   at your feet,
  you perch yourself
    on the stool,
smiling broadly, as you
        say,
   'have i ever told you the
    story
  about 2 boys
      and their daddy?'

Second Sunday of Advent

splendiferous

On the glorious splendor of
    your majesty,
  and on your wondrous
    works, I will meditate. (Psalm 145:5)

i stand at the edge
      of the Grand Canyon,
  i look at towering Everest
    behind Hillary and Norgay,
      i shudder at the approaching
dust storm in the Southwest:
      the wonders of your
    creation - their power and force,
      their majesty and imagination
  can stun me into silent awe . . .

but it is when i puzzle over
    the ability of a cat
  to remain perfectly still
      for hours, that
    i learn of your patience;
it is when i notice
      a little boy
  give half of his lunch
    to a homeless man
      on the park bench
  that i see your face;
it is when i pay attention
      to the wordless lullaby
  a mother sings to
      her sick child
    in the hospital, that
  i hear your voice;

it is at the end
      of the day, when
  i mull over all the simple
        things
  i encountered, that
      i realize the intricacies
  of your heart.

Second Monday of Advent

which?

"*Teacher, which commandment in the law is the greatest?*" *He said to him, "'You shall love the Lord your God with all your heart, and with all your soul, and with all your mind.' This is the greatest and first commandment. And a second is like it: 'You shall love your neighbor as yourself.' On these two commandments hang all the law and the prophets.*" (Matthew 22:36-40)

    i have not
        committed murder,
            though
     if thoughts could
          kill . . .

    i don't take what
        isn't mine (at least,
      while anyone
           is watching);

    i don't bear false
        witness
      against my friends
   (you're not counting
         gossip,
      are you?);

    i remain faithful
        as i can be
   (looking, but not touching,
         is permissible, is my
         understanding);

    i value my parents
        as much as
        anyone else, even
     though i may not call
     as often as i could;

i don't misuse your
        Name (except when
  i stub my toe in the dark,
  miss an appointment,
  get cut off in traffic, but
    i trust you know i don't
    mean anything by it!)

but actually love

                you,

    others,

            myself?

Second Tuesday of Advent

the oath

When I saw him, I fell at his feet as though dead. But he placed his right hand on me, saying, "Do not be afraid; I am the first and the last, and the living one. I was dead, and see, I am alive forever and ever; and I have the keys of Death and of Hades." (Revelation 1:17-18)

you whisper the
        promise
    as we take our
      first breath,
our lungs expanding
  with Spirit's gift;

you put your arms
     around us,
         murmuring
as you gently
       bandage our
  souls from
sin's bullying;

you write the
      words
  on a piece of
    paper,
putting it in our
    lunchbox
  on that first day
    of school;

you shout it
at the top of your
       lungs,
  when we are
    deafened
  by the decibel-breaking
     din of the
  world;

you sigh the
          promise
  as we take our
      last breath,
    the Spirit cradling us
    to carry us home to
          you:

"do not be afraid"

Second Wednesday of Advent

neglect

"Woe to you, scribes and Pharisees, hypocrites! For you tithe mint, dill, and cummin, and have neglected the weightier matters of the law: justice and mercy and faith. It is these you ought to have practiced without neglecting the others." (Matthew 23:23)

when my alma mater
    calls, i have
       in mind what
          i will give
         this year;

when the community fund
    cards are handed
    out at work, i know
what the bosses
   expect (100% participation,
      $$$ isn't primary);

when the preacher stands
   up on stewardship
      Sunday,
i already have the pledge
   filled out (same
  as last year, thank you!)

but

do i fight for justice
    for only a tenth
 of the people who need it?

do i carefully measure out
   10% of mercy (when
i expect 115% for
     myself)?

do i simply tithe my
    faith, especially
  since i have so little
to begin with?

Second Thursday of Advent

praise!

Praise the LORD*!*
Praise the LORD *from the heavens;*
  praise him in the heights!
Praise him, all his angels;
  praise him, all his host!
Praise him, sun and moon;
  praise him, all you shining stars!
Praise him, you highest heavens,
  and you waters above the heavens!
Let them praise the name of the LORD*,*
  for he commanded and they were created. (Psalm 148:1-5)

little kids
  who sing carols with their
      hands
and grandparents
  living in their childhood
        Christmases;
geese announcing
    their departure times,
and chickadees ice skating
    in birdbaths;
giraffes craning
    their necks towards
    the winter moon,
and bears hibernating
    in winter's cradle;
hawks soaring
    higher and higher
    in the sky,
and rabbits burrowing
    deeper and deeper;
cats meditating
    for hours on end,
dogs excitedly
   letting us know
   another snowfall has
        arrived;

all creation:
  Praise!

Second Friday of Advent

now

The prayers of David son of Jesse are ended. (Psalm 72:20)

so
    now
  it is our turn
   to pray

that those who
    hunger
  for justice
   will be fed
    fairly;

that those who
   wander need's streets
  will find someone
   to lead them
    to help;

that those so weakened
   by life's blows
    will be gathered up
  and strengthened by
   grace and hope;

that we face down
      oppression
  and kick it out of
   town;

that our prayers have
  hands
   feet
    backbones
   minds
  courage.

Second Saturday of Advent

students

Good and upright is the L<small>ORD</small>;
*　　therefore he instructs sinners in the way.*
He leads the humble in what is right,
*　　and teaches the humble his way.*
All the paths of the L<small>ORD</small> are
*　　steadfast love and faithfulness,*
*　　for those who keep his covenant*
*　　　　and his decrees. (Psalm 25:8-10)*

arriving late
　　for Humility 101,
　i slip into the back
　　　　row, hoping
　　you will not notice;

putting my notepad
　　　on the desk,
　i hold my pen to the
　　　　paper, so
　that it looks like i
　am paying rapt attention
　　　　and taking copious notes;

i make sure to keep my
　　　　eyes wide open
　and glued to the board
　　where you are showing
　　　　the formula
　on how the last become first, all the while
　daydreaming of the warm bed
　　　i just left;

at the end of class,
　　i turn towards the place
　　where i can get a refill
　　on my latte grande,
　　never noticing my mates
　following you to the corner
　　　　of
　Steadfast Love
　　　And Faithfulness.

Third Sunday of Advent

tetchy

*I waited patiently for the
    LORD;* (Psalm 40:1a)

questioning who
        i might have been
    if God had only
            granted me
    the gifts i hunger for . . .

imagining what
        life might be like
    if God had given me
            a different family . . .

thinking about how
            much i could do
    for others
            if God would only
    let me win the
                lottery . . .

wondering why
        it is taking God
    so long to catch up
            with me as
    i race towards my foolish
            goals . . .

. . . i wait
            impatiently
    for the Lord.

Third Monday of Advent

bear hug

Steadfast love and
    faithfulness will meet;
righteousness and peace
    will kiss each other.
Faithfulness will spring up
    from the ground,
and righteousness will
    look down from the
    sky. (Psalm 85:10-11)

like the full moon
   floating across
   winter's sky,
       righteousness
     looks upon us,
     brightening the shadows
       of our
  bleakness;

like old friends
   at an airport meeting
   after years apart,
       faithfulness and peace
     wrap us in a great
     bear hug which
       will never
  let go;

like a
crossing guard
   who steps into the
   busy traffic so we
   get to the other side,
       steadfast love
     watches over us
       in every
  moment.

Third Tuesday of Advent

blankly

They heard the sound of the L{\scriptsize ORD} God walking in the garden at the time of the evening breeze, and the man and his wife hid themselves from the presence of the L{\scriptsize ORD} God among the trees of the garden. But the L{\scriptsize ORD} God called to the man, and said to him, "Where are you?" He said, "I heard the sound of you in the garden, and I was afraid, because I was naked; and I hid myself." (Genesis 3:8-10)

i want to
    walk with you
    by my side,
        but i am
        fearful
that you might want
to go to _____;

i long to
    to talk with you,
    to hear your voice,
        but what if
        you ask me
to _____ or
_____ or
(heaven forbid!)
_____?

i hope that
    you are always
    watching over me,
but you don't mind
    if i occasionally
shut the door,
draw the drapes,
close the blinds while i
    _____?

Third Wednesday of Advent

the elect

Paul, a servant of God and an apostle of Jesus Christ, for the sake of the faith of God's elect and the knowledge of the truth that is in accordance with godliness, (Titus 1:1)

the broken
    no one will
 fix

the lost
    we offer no
 directions

the hungry
    who are not
    given even the
    scraps from our
 tables

the outcast
    we dare not
 touch

the fallen
    we refuse to
 lift up

in God's eyes,
    these are the
 elect

      the favored ones.

Third Thursday of Advent

inheritance

Let this be recorded for a
*   generation to come,*
* so that a people yet unborn*
*   may praise the* LORD*:*
that he looked down from
*   his holy height,*
* from heaven the* LORD
*   looked at the earth,*
to hear the groans of the
*   prisoners,*
to set free those who were
*   doomed to die;*
so that the name of the LORD
*   may be declared in*
*   Zion,*
* and his praise in*
*   Jerusalem,*
when peoples gather
*   together,*
* and kingdoms, to worship*
*   the* LORD*.* (Psalm 102:18-22)

not grand
    cathedrals
  but the rubble
    of all the walls
    built to keep
      others out;

not mighty pipe
    organs
  and fine
    cantatas,
  but the silenced
  songs of all those
    on the 'wrong'
      side;

not thick theological
           treatises,
     but the crayon
     drawings of the
           child rescued
     from her life of
                abuse;

not our framed
           diplomas
     and retirement
           mementos,
     but the names
     of those who
           transformed our
     lives by their
                humility -

let these be
     the inheritance
     we pass on
           and on . . .

Third Friday of Advent

in every season

This Spirit he poured out on us richly through Jesus Christ our Savior, so that, having been justified by his grace, we might become heirs according to the hope of eternal life. (Titus 3:6-7)

like a spring
      shower,
  may the Spirit
   bring forth new
        life
    in us;

like the spray
  from the hose
      on a hot summer
   day, may the Spirit
  send us jumping and
     laughing with
       delight;

like an autumn
        storm,
  may the Spirit
   rattle our souls
and awaken us
    from our
  apathy;

like a warm bath
    on an icy
   winter night,
      may the Spirit
cradle us with the
    carols of
      holiness;

in every season
       of our lives,
  drench us with the
    Spirit!

Third Saturday of Advent

i'm dreaming of

But just when he had resolved to do this, an angel of the Lord appeared to him in a dream and said, "Joseph, son of David, do not be afraid to take Mary as your wife, for the child conceived in her is from the Holy Spirit." (Matthew 1:20)

cities
    where building homes
        for families
    on the street are
    more important than
      sports arenas;

neighborhoods
    filled with
  children from every
    place on earth,
      playing
  together in peace;

streets
    which do not
        welcome
    drug dealers and
    gun wielders;

homes
    where residents
        live out
  justice,
    peace,
      and hope;

people
    who love more
      than hate,
    give more than
        take,
    share more
      than hoard.

Fourth Sunday of Advent

impatiently

*I wait for the L*ORD*, my soul*
*   waits,*
* and in his word I hope;*
my soul waits for the Lord
* more than those who*
*   watch for the morning,*
* more than those who*
*   watch for the morning.* (Psalm 130:5-6)

with a PhD in
      procrastination
  it is not hard
  for me to
    wait

so in the
  crush of
last-minute
     shoppers
    i wait . . .

   to catch a glimpse
  of you

in the
  din of too loud
     too often
    and too many
holiday songs
    i wait . . .

   to hear you
    whisper my name

in the
    stopped traffic
  the crisp air
    shimmering with
   exhaust fumes
     i wait . . .

to draw closer
   to you

in this season of
   impatience,

i wait . . .

Fourth Monday of Advent

freedom

The LORD sets the prisoners
    free;
  the LORD opens the eyes of
    the blind.
The LORD lifts up those who
    are bowed down;
  the LORD loves the
    righteous.
The LORD watches over the
    strangers; (Psalm 146:7c-9a)

when i am tempted
    to place myself
      in bondage to debt
  in order to show
  how much i love
      others,

  set me free
    to give them
    myself
      instead;

when the glitter,
    the tinsel,
  all the bright shiny
    got-to-have-or-elses
      cause me to
        squeeze my eyes
          tight shut,

  open them, so
  i can see the
    snow falling gently
    on a winter's night;

when i can only
    think that all
    the names on
  all the lists
    are the only ones
    that matter,

may the shepherds
stop me to tell
  (with wonder and
    delight
and just a smidgen
    of mystery)
     of the little
       stranger
they just met
in a barn.

Fourth Tuesday of Advent

advent eyes

*As for me, I shall behold
    your face in
    righteousness;
  when I awake I shall be
    satisfied, beholding
    your likeness.* (Psalm 17:15)

in the little
    child
saying his prayers,
    i see your
        trust;

in the old
    man
sitting by the bed
in the hospice,
    i see your
        hope;

in my
    partner
smiling at me
as i open my eyes
each morning,
    i see your
        faithfulness;

in the tiny
    baby
born in a barn,
    i behold your
        love.

Fourth Wednesday of Advent

so many

Praise the LORD,
   O Jerusalem!
Praise your God, O Zion! (Psalm 147:12)

as icy bitterness gusts and swirls
   around them, the doves huddle together,
   clinging tightly to the wires
   humming with power, until
      suddenly
   they dart up in a great cloud, first
      flapping and spiraling,
      then gliding, in the
      winter sky, in delight;

little kids
   leave the room
   a giggled shambles,
   as they carry the presents
   wrapped in mismatched
   paper, held together
      with so much tape two
      scissors will be needed, and
   place them at the
   back of the tree,
      with whispered joy;

grandparents walking
      hand-in-hand
   on snow littered sidewalks,
      noticing who has a different tree
      this year,
   which prodigal's reflection is seen
      in the window-framed glow,
   who has welcomed
   the immigrant family
      to the annual
      wine-and-cheese gathering;

so many ways to
   praise,
we'll never run out.

Fourth Thursday of Advent

but

If you, O LORD, should mark
    iniquities,
Lord, who could stand?
But there is forgiveness with
    you,
  so that you may be
    revered. (Psalm 130:3-4)

you write
    down our every
  fault, always
using invisible ink;

you video-tape
    our every
  vanity, forgetting
to press the **record**
    button;

you could bury
    all manner of
  grudges deep
  in the hollows
  of your heart,

but you
    empty
 it

into the cracks
of our lives
to make us
    whole.

Fourth Friday of Advent

night silence

Let the same mind be in you that was in Christ Jesus,
  who, though he was in the
    form of God,
  did not regard equality
    with God
  as something to be
    exploited,
 but emptied himself,
    taking the form of a slave,
    being born in human
     likeness.
 And being found in human
   form,
 he humbled himself
 and became obedient to
   the point of death--
 even death on a cross. (Philippians 2:5-8)

in the night's
     silence,
  while we slept dreaming
      of all
   that awaited us
     under the tree,
you
    crept down
  out of heaven,
     so softly no
   motion detector
  could go off

to burrow
   under the covers
 with us, swaddling
    us with peace
    given for all,
  your grace
    warming our
     cold feet
 until we giggled
     with delight.

    Christmas Eve

one

The one who comes from above is above all; the one who is of the earth belongs to the earth and speaks about earthly things. The one who comes from heaven is above all. He testifies to what he has seen and heard, yet no one accepts his testimony. Whoever has accepted his testimony has certified this, that God is true. He whom God has sent speaks the words of God, for he gives the Spirit without measure. The Father loves the Son and has placed all things in his hands.
(John 3:31-35)

you came,
    not for the carols
        sung by candlelight

    but so we
could hear the
broken lullabies
  of parents who
  work a double shift
     while their children
     are asleep;

you came
    not for homilies
    and meditations (however
        perfectly polished)

    but so we
might stammer
    the good news
that our lives of service
        and humility
  speak louder
  than any words;

you came
    not so we
        would
    isolate ourselves
    with parties and
        pageants,

             but so we
         might enact
                    the mystery
               of your coming,
            with deeds of
                            justice and
                         peace

for every

one.

Christmas Day

Thom M. Shuman is a graduate of Eckerd College (St. Petersburg, FL) and Union Presbyterian Seminary (Richmond, VA). Currently active in transitional/interim ministry, he has served churches in Oklahoma, Virginia, and Ohio. His liturgies, poems, and prayers are used by congregations all over the world, and by individuals for personal devotions.

His Advent devotional books *The Jesse Tree* (2005) and *Gobsmacked* (2011) have been published by Wild Goose Publications/The Iona Community (www.ionabooks.com), as well as his wedding liturgy, *Now Come Two Hearts*. Wild Goose has also published e-liturgies for Ascension Day, the Day of Transfiguration, Ash Wednesday, Maundy Thursday, and Good Friday. In addition, they have published *Companions for the Journey* (a blessing of animals), *Advent Nudges, Lenten and Easter Nudges,* and *A Lenten and Easter Cycle.* He is also a contributor to the Iona Community's Resource books *Candles & Conifers, Hay & Stardust, Fire and Bread, Bare Feet and Buttercups,* and *Acorns and Archangels*, as well as *Going Home Another Way: Daily Readings and Resources for Christmastide, Gathered and Scattered: Readings and Meditations from the Iona Community, 50 New Prayers From The Iona Community,* and *Like Leaves to the Sun, Prayers from the Iona Community.*

He is the author of *Playing Hopscotch in Heaven, Lectionary Liturgies for RCL Year A,* as well as its companion book, *Piano Man, Poems and Prayers for Lectionary Year A; Where the Broken Gather* (liturgies) and *Dust Shaker* (poems and prayers) are based on the readings for RCL Year B. *Bearers of Grace and Justice* (liturgies) and *Pirate Jesus* (poems and prayers) are for RCL Year C. All are available from Amazon.

Dusty the Church Dog and other sightings of the gospel is also available from Amazon.

He blogs at www.occasionalsightings.blogspot.com
www.prayersfortoday.blogspot.com
www.lectionaryliturgies.blogspot.com

Extracts from the New Revised Standard Version © Copyright © 1989, by the Division of Christian Education of the National Council of the Churches of Christ in the United States of America. Used by permission. All rights reserved.

Printed in Great Britain
by Amazon